BRITAIN'S ♜ HERITAGE

British Military Jets

Kev Darling

AMBERLEY

First published 2017

Amberley Publishing
The Hill, Stroud
Gloucestershire, GL5 4EP

www.amberley-books.com

Copyright © Kev Darling, 2017

The right of Kev Darling to be identified as
the Author of this work has been asserted in
accordance with the Copyrights, Designs and
Patents Act 1988.

ISBN 978 1 4456 6932 8 (paperback)
ISBN 978 1 4456 6933 5 (ebook)

British Library Cataloguing in Publication Data.
A catalogue record for this book is available from
the British Library.

Printed in the UK.

Contents

1
Introduction: From Hot War to Cold War

'The enemy of my enemy is my friend.' So runs the ancient saying that bound the Western Allies together with their erstwhile Russian counterparts. This uneasy coalition remained active until the cessation of hostilities in 1945. Russia, under the control of a very suspicious Josef Stalin, quickly broke up this partnership and decided to retain all of the territories in Eastern Europe and the Baltic states.

Having discarded all of the treaties discussed during the Second World War it was obvious that Stalin had his eye on further incursions into Europe. Fearful that such advances would be made, the countries of Western Europe plus America, Britain and Canada formed the Western Union to guard against such possibilities. Not long after the Berlin Blockade in 1948 the North Atlantic Treat Organisation, NATO, came into being, emerging from the Treaty of Brussels in 1949. Consisting of all the Western European nations plus America, Britain and Canada, this collective would face up to the Russian-sponsored Warsaw Pact that emerged 1955.

Looking decidedly tatty is this Avro Vulcan B.2 XL320 of the Scampton Wing. In the bombs bay is a Blue Steel missile that was Britain's nuclear deterrent until the submarine-launched Polaris took over the task in 1970. (NARA via Dennis R Jenkins)

All of this manoeuvring would lead to the creation of 'The Iron Curtain'; on one side were those countries under the thrall of the Soviet Union while on the other were those of the Western powers. To further create a feeling of separation, the Berlin Wall was built across Berlin and out into the surrounding countryside, construction beginning in 1961. The edifice itself lasted until 1989 when the Warsaw Pact collapsed under its own inertia.

From the British point of view the answer was to develop a range of jet aircraft: their purpose was to defend the country and carry the war to the newly emerged aggressor. Not only were new aircraft on the drawing board, but nuclear weapons came to the fore. Fortunately British scientists had worked on the Manhattan Project, the American atomic bomb, and were well aware of the techniques required to create such a weapon. This small tome covers those British-designed and built combat aircraft that stood between safety and total destruction.

Did you know?

The NATO/Warsaw Pact standoff relied on the MAD policy, Mutually Assured Destruction. And pure madness it was too – nobody would win except the cockroaches. Each side invested millions in developing weapons and undertaking various forms of spying to either acquire unavailable technologies or to see what the other side was up to. Although no actual combat took place, thankfully, there were some incidents that resulted in casualties.

Throttles fully forward, Valiant BK.1 XD816 powers towards the camera. The fin badge is that of the Marham Wing. Transferred to BAC, the airframe was used for various trials before being grounded in 1970. (AviPix)

2

Here Come the Hot Jets

Do you remember Frank Whittle? Or Hans Joachim Pabst von Ohain? Both were responsible for the most significant invention of the twentieth century: the jet engine. Frank, later Sir Frank, Whittle joined the RAF as an apprentice in 1923. Such were his academic and practical skills that he quickly qualified as a pilot at Cranwell in 1928. The Whittle motorjet engine was submitted as the core of his graduation thesis and would, after much development, become known as the centrifugal jet engine. This idea was patented in 1930.

Across the North Sea in Germany von Ohain was also looking at the jet engine. Like many good ideas, it took some time to gain traction, although Ernst Heinkel agreed to have an airframe built to house the new powerplant. The resultant airframe, the Heinkel He 178, made its maiden flight with the Ohain turbojet installed in 1939, while the Whittle engine made its maiden flight in the Gloster E.29/39 in 1941. Although there were problems with the Ohain engine, various German manufacturers were starting to progress along a different path toward the axial flow compressor engine, better known today as the turbojet and its bigger brother the turbofan.

RAF Fighter Command had embraced the jet fighter very early on in its career. Success with the Gloster Whittle powered by a Whittle/Power Jets engine had led to the development and deployment of the Meteor F.1. Deliveries of the first production machines, later to be named Meteor, took place in July 1944 with 616 Squadron being the recipient. Powered by Welland engines, the new fighter was deployed on V.1 'Doodle Bug' interception patrols. While the majority of the squadron remained in Britain one flight was detached to the Netherlands, although the Meteor was banned from flying over enemy territory; thus two of the most significant aircraft in jet aircraft development failed to meet in combat.

Seen taking off on an early test flight is the Gloster E.28/39 'Whittle', built to test the Frank Whittle centrifugal engine. W4041/G currently resides in the Science Museum in London. (AviPix)

Currently lurking in the RAF Museum is this early Meteor prototype, DG202/G. Throughout the war period this aircraft was heavily involved in trials work before being withdrawn from active use in 1945. (AviPix)

Pictured at St Athan is this very special Meteor F.4. EE549 would be flown by Group Captain Teddy Donaldson of the High Speed Flight to achieve a new speed record of 615 mph on 7 September 1946. (AviPix)

This first marque was followed by the Meteor F.3 with various improvements, including higher-thrust, more reliable engines, a ventral fuel tank plus a sliding canopy. 616 Squadron would be the first recipient with 504 Squadron receiving their aircraft soon afterwards. The follow-on would be the Meteor F.4, this being the first version to enter mass squadron service; a total of twenty-four units flew this model. 92 Squadron would be the first to equip, in May 1948 while based at Duxford, while 245 Squadron would achieve a measure of fame when some of their machines were fitted with refuelling probes for refuelling trials.

Having delivered these early Meteors, Gloster would then go on to manufacture the most numerous version, the Meteor F.8, with a total of 1,079 aircraft being delivered. In contrast to the earlier machines the F.8 featured an extended nose, clipped wings, modified tail unit and a Martin-Baker ejection seat. At its height the F.8 equipped thirty squadrons, including ten assigned to the Royal Auxiliary Air Force. The final front-line Meteor F.8 was retired by 245 Squadron in April 1957.

Also in the race to deliver the first jet fighter to the RAF was de Havilland with its Spidercrab, later given the more sensible service name of Vampire. The powerplant

Above: Carrying the unit bars of No. 615 Squadron is Gloster Meteor F.8 VZ467/01. By this time the Meteor was bring operated by Brawdy Station Flight. (AviPix)

Below: Sporting the unit markings of No. 56 Squadron, this Meteor F.8, WK991, had served with 46 Squadron for target towing duties, which lasted until 1959. It is possible to visit this aircraft at IWM Duxford. (AviPix)

for this diminutive fighter would be the Halford H.1 designed by Major Frank Halford. This was a simpler and slightly smaller version of the Welland engines specified for the Gloster Meteor. The first DH.100, LZ548/G, undertook its maiden flight in September 1943, some six months after its Gloster rival had flown. In appearance the Vampire series was a small single-seat twin-boom fighter that still featured wood in much of its construction. The pilot plus engine were housed in a short pod, as were four 20 mm cannon.

The first production Vampire F.1, TG274, made its maiden flight in April 1945 with first deliveries being undertaken to 247 Squadron during March 1946. Changes took place throughout delivery, thus from the fortieth aircraft a more powerful Goblin, as the Halford H.1 had become, was fitted, while from the fifty-first aircraft the F.1 featured a bubble canopy and cabin pressurisation. Eventually a total of eleven front-line units were equipped with this model. Given its diminutive size, it was no surprise that the short endurance of the Vampire needed to be addressed quickly; therefore the next model would be the F.3. Although underwing tanks had been introduced with the F.1, this later version also had increased tankage in the wings. In its initial iteration the extra wing fuel caused some instability that was cured by lowering the tailplane and extending its chord while the fin and rudder were reworked to increase the surface area. The first prototype first flew in November 1945, with first deliveries being undertaken to 54 Squadron in April 1948. Eventually a total of thirteen units were equipped with the type.

While the Vampire proved to be a stable platform it was obvious that any further development as a fighter would be limited by its size, thus any further models would be dedicated to ground attack only. To that end de Havilland reworked an F.1 as the FB.5 prototype. To cope with the differing demands of the ground attack role, the new model featured a strengthened structure that allowed the carriage of two 1,000 lb bombs or eight rockets. The prototype undertook its maiden flight in June 1948 with deliveries to the first operational squadron taking place soon afterwards. Eventually a total of forty-one squadrons were equipped with this model. The final Vampire fighter bomber was the FB.9, which was intended for tropical usage, adding a conditioning unit to the basic FB.5 airframe. First deliveries were undertaken during January 1952. Overall twenty-four fighter bomber units were equipped with this version.

De Havilland Vampire F.1 TG278 was the fifth production machine and was initially used for test flying. In March 1948 the fighter, heavily modified, achieved a height record of 59,445.5 feet, piloted by Group Captain John Cunningham. (AviPix)

The de Havilland Vampire NF.10 night fighter was a stopgap fitted with the AI Mk 10 radar. The first production aircraft entered service in July 1951, with the type remaining in use until 1954 and being operated by three squadrons. De Havilland would also be the manufacturers of the Venom NF.2 and NF.3 night fighters. Based on the earlier FB.1 Venom, the NF versions featured an extended and enlarged pod that housed the pilot and navigator/radar operator on side-by-side seating while the radar unit was mounted in the extreme nose. As with the earlier Vampire NF.10, the armament of four 20 mm cannon was carried in the nose. A total of sixty Venom NF.2s were eventually delivered

Above: The violent face of the Vampire: its quartet of four 20mm Hispano cannon. When the Vampire was converted to the ground attack role, rockets and bombs were added to its repertoire. (AviPix)
Below: DH Vampire FB.5 WA331, flown by the Commanding Officer of No. 112 Squadron, based at Fassberg, Germany – hence the colourful fin markings. A preserved Vampire FB.5 can be seen at RAF Museum Cosford. (AviPix)

to Fighter Command. Following on from the Venom NF.2 came the NF.3; this featured an improved radar, power-operated ailerons to improve manoeuvrability at high altitude, redesigned rudder surfaces, a frameless canopy to improve all-round visibility plus ejection seats. A total of 129 aircraft were built, the first having made its maiden flight in February 1953. The NF.2 was flown by four squadrons while the NF.3 was flown by five squadrons.

Operating alongside the de Havilland Venom were the night fighter versions of the Gloster Meteor. As Gloster were overloaded with producing the day fighters, the construction of these aircraft was transferred to another company within the Hawker group, Armstrong Whitworth. The first version, the Meteor NF.11, featured an elongated nose that housed the pilot and navigator plus the radar system, this being the Westinghouse SCR-720. The wings were of the long span variety from the early fighter models; this gave the aircraft greater stability at altitude. As the nose was occupied by the radar, the cannon armament was relocated into the wings, while fuel was increased by the addition of underwing tanks and a ventral tank. The prototype Meteor NF.11 undertook its maiden flight in May 1950 while the first production machine flew the following November. Eventually 358 aircraft were manufactured, most of which served with the Royal Air Force. This marque would serve with fourteen squadrons. The Meteor NF.11 remained in operational usage until replaced by the Javelin in June 1960.

The following version was the NF.12 that was a development of the NF.11, although this featured an American-supplied APS 21 radar that required a further fuselage extension. Eventually a total of 100 aircraft were built and served with eight squadrons. The final model of the Meteor night fighter was the NF.14, of which 100 were manufactured. The first NF.14 undertook its maiden flight in October 1953 while the last was delivered in May 1954. The NF.14 differed from the earlier models as it featured an even longer nose that housed the American-built AN/APQ-43 radar, while to maintain stability yaw dampers were fitted to the rudder. The most visible change, however, was the canopy, which was completely clear – this replacing the previously framed assemblies. Although the NF.14 left front-line service in 1961 when replaced by the Javelin, it did serve with twelve squadrons.

Awaiting its crew is Vampire NF.10 WP256 of No. 23 Squadron, based at Coltishall. When it was introduced the NF.10 could easily catch the bombers of Bomber Command. This pushed forward the need for the Canberra, which could escape from the Vampire. (AviPix)

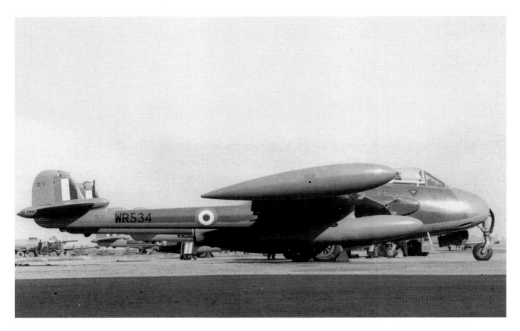

Above: When the DH Venom FB.4 entered service with the RAF it was a vast improvement on the earlier FB.1, which was very unstable in flight. WR534 was operated in the fighter bomber role in the Middle East. (AviPix)

Below: The night version of the Venom FB.4 was the NF.3. WX838 was assigned to No. 141 Squadron, based at RAF Wittering, where it replaced the Meteor NF.11 and was in turn replaced by the Gloster Javelin. (AviPix)

Not normally seen in daylight hours is this Gloster Meteor NF.14, WS775, as this version was intended for night fighter use. This particular aircraft served with No. 85 Squadron. (AviPix)

Did you know?

Both the Meteor and Vampire achieved quantity sales overseas, not only within Europe but to other countries such as Rhodesia where they were extensively modified to carry a greater weapons load.

3
Going Faster

It had become obvious by 1953 that the Meteor and Vampire had been totally outclassed by the emerging crop of Russian fighters. Unfortunately, the next British fighter was still in the development stage; therefore a stopgap was needed in a hurry. The only available candidate was the North American F-86E Sabre, which had already proven its worth in Korea. It would be Canadair who would build the RAF fighters under license. Altogether some 430 aircraft were built for Britain, these being flown across the Atlantic by pilots from No. 1 (Long Range) Ferry Unit as part of Operation Bechers Brook. While the majority of the new fighters were delivered to the units based in Germany, two units in Fighter Command were equipped with the type, these being 66 and 92 Squadrons. The F-86 Sabre F.4 was withdrawn from service in 1956, the majority being refurbished for further use by other nations.

The first British swept-wing fighter to enter service was the Supermarine Swift. The Swift was an unmitigated disaster in its earliest form. The first Swift F.1 undertook its maiden flight in August 1952. This version had a pair of 30 mm Aden cannon, a fixed tailplane plus a Rolls-Royce Avon engine without reheat. Development problems delayed service entry until February 1954, when 56 Squadron traded in its trusty Gloster

The early versions of the Supermarine Swift were withdrawn from service for being dangerous. The only marque to enter service in any numbers was the Swift FR.5, operated by Nos 2 and 79 Squadrons. (AviPix)

Meteor F.8s. The pilots were then faced by an aircraft that was beset by flight restrictions that affected gun firing, maximum speed and altitude. This was compounded by a spate of accidents that caused the type to be grounded in August of that year. By the end of that month the squadron had received the next model, the Swift F.2, which was supposed to be a better aircraft. Unfortunately the opposite was true, as two aircraft were lost due to un-commanded pitch ups. By this time the RAF had lost patience and ordered the withdrawal of the fleet from flying in March 1955. Only one version would enter unit service in appreciable numbers, this being the Swift FR.5 that would operate with 2 and 79 Squadrons in Germany.

It would be the Hawker Aircraft Company that would produce the next RAF fighter, the Hunter. The first Hunter F.1, WT555, undertook its maiden flight in May 1953, this being followed by a total of 113 aircraft from Kingston while a further twenty-six were built at the Blackpool factory. Flight testing would show that a ventral airbrake was needed to improve handling, which delayed service entry until July 1954. 43 Squadron would be the first to equip, being quickly followed by 54 and 222 Squadrons. While the looks were graceful, this first model did suffer some problems, the greatest of which was engine surging at high altitude when the guns were fired; also, the links ejected during gun firing caused damage to the aircraft's skin. The next Avon-powered Hunter to enter service would be the F.4, this having increased fuel in the wing while the airframe was capable of carrying a far greater weapons load under the wings. The first F.4 undertook its maiden flight in October 1954 with 188 being built at Kingston while a further 177 were constructed at Blackpool. The F.4 entered service with 54 and 111 Squadrons in March 1955. Eventually a total of twenty-three squadrons would equip with the Hunter.

The Hawker Hunter was a quantum leap in performance from earlier jet aircraft. This F.6A sports the nose bars and badges of No. 234 Squadron. The F.6A was capable of carrying numerous weapons under the wings that included bombs and rockets. (AviPix)

Following on from the F.6 Hunter was the FGA.9. This added a tail brake chute in a fairing above the jet pipe plus strengthened wings for increased weapons carriage. In this view the XG226 sports the markings of No. 79 Squadron. (AviPix)

The definitive fighter, the Hunter F.6, would make its first flight in January 1954 with 264 being built. The first production model flew in March 1955, these being matched by a further 119 machines built by Armstrong Whitworth. As production progressed the aircraft were fitted with an extended wing outer section that improved handling, while the gun links would be collected in blisters under the gun pack. The final F.6 was delivered in July 1957. Eventually twenty front-line fighter units were equipped with this model and after leaving service it saw extensive used by second-line units.

The final Avon-powered version of the Hunter delivered to the RAF was the FGA.9 that, as its designation shows, was dedicated to the ground attack role. Based on the earlier F.6, the first aircraft, XE617, undertook its maiden flight in July 1959. Modifications applied to this model included a tail brake parachute compartment above the jet pipe fairing, the fitting of 230-gallon underwing tanks on the inboard pylons plus strengthened wings capable of carrying an increased weapons load, improved cockpit ventilation and air conditioning. Eventually, nine squadrons of Fighter Command were equipped with this version although the greater majority were delivered to the various overseas commands.

Two other Hunter versions were manufactured, these being the F.2 and F.5. The primary difference between this and the other models was the fitting of a Sapphire engine – the intention being to give the Hunter another powerplant should there be a shortfall in Avon manufacture. The Hunter F.2 was manufactured by Armstrong Whitworth, with forty-five being built. Only two units would be equipped, these being 257 and 263 Squadrons. The

Above: Outside of Britain the Hunter FGA.9 found combat usage in the Middle East. Here XK151/D of No. 8 Squadron taxies in at Khormaksar, Aden, during the trouble there. (AviPix)
Below: Sporting nose bars and the Phoenix badge on its nose plus red and white squares on the wing tips is this Hunter F.6 of No. 56 Squadron at Wattisham. (AviPix)

The Hunter FR.10 was developed to replace the Supermarine Swift FR.5 in the reconnaissance role. XE585 would be assigned to No. 2 Squadron in Germany. After RAF service the airframe was refurbished and sold to the Indian Air Force. (AviPix)

next model would be the F.5, which was equivalent to the Avon-powered F.4 and would be delivered to six front-line units. Both of the Sapphire-powered versions would be withdrawn from use by 1958, although the F.5 would see action during the Suez Crisis in 1956.

While the RAF was reasonably well equipped with day fighter aircraft, there was a greater need for an aircraft that could operate in all weathers and at night. The Javelin would be the first delta-wing twin-engined fighter in the world. The aircraft was designed to have high performance, good endurance and be capable of intercepting incoming bombers flying at high altitudes and high subsonic speeds. The onboard avionics had to be capable of detecting intruders in all weathers at either night or day.

The first Javelin prototype, WD804, undertook its maiden flight from the company airfield at Moreton Valance in November 1951, being followed by a further two machines. The third aircraft, WT827, was the first to be fitted with the intended gun armament, four 30 mm cannon. The test flights of the prototypes did reveal some instability during parts of the flight regime, although these were quickly cured by modifying the wing. The first production aircraft, XA544, flew in October 1955, although service entry was delayed due to accidents suffered by the prototypes. Eventually 46 Squadron received their allocation from the forty built in February 1956. These machines were powered by Sapphire Sa6 engines while the radar was the A117 unit. Only one other squadron would receive the FAW.1, this being the Germany-based 87 Squadron.

The initial FAW.1 was quickly followed by the FAW.2, of which thirty were built. These were similar to the preceding version, although the radar was the American-built AI22 unit.

Captured at RAF Stradishall is Gloster Javelin FAW.6 XA815 of No. 89 Squadron. The squadron flew the Javelin for two years before it was renumbered as No. 85 Squadron during a period of air force contraction. (AviPix)

Three squadrons would be equipped with this version. In September 1955 the next version of the Javelin undertook its maiden flight, this being the FAW.4. This marque differed from the previous aircraft in that it featured an all flying tailplane for pitch control. Only fifty FAW.4s were built, these being operated by eight squadrons at various times. The FAW.4 was quickly followed by the FAW.5, the major change applied to this version being the incorporation of extra wing tankage that increased available fuel by a further 250 gallons. Squadrons were issued with the FAW.5.

The following version was the FAW.6, this incorporating all of the previous modifications applied to the preceding models. The FAW.6, of which thirty-three were constructed, was fitted with the American-built AI22 radar and would be issued to the same units that were flying the FAW.2, both types being operated concurrently.

The arrival of the FAW.7 was a quantum leap over the earlier marques as it featured Sapphire engines of increased thrust. Provision for drop tanks was built into each wing pylon while the rear fuselage was extended to cope with the revised engine exhausts. Changes were also made to the wings as vortex generators were fitted to the outer wing panels while the ailerons had their trailing edges thickened. The armament was also updated to include the Firestreak air-to-air missile and it was intended to reduce the number of cannon to two, although due to delays in the missile's development early aircraft were delivered with the original quartet of cannon installed.

The final production Javelin to be produced was the FAW.8, which featured Sapphire engines with limited reheat while the radar employed was the American AI.22 that was coupled to a Sperry auto-pilot. The FAW.8 also featured a revised wing complete with a drooped leading edge and a double row of vortex generators, while the flight control surfaces were fitted with yaw and pitch dampers. While the limited reheat was of value at high altitude, its operation at lower altitudes caused a loss of thrust. The first airframe undertook its maiden flight in May 1958, a total of forty-seven being built. When the final FAW.8 rolled out of the door it was in fact the last machine to be built at the Gloster factory, although modification and repair would keep the work force in business for a few more years. Only two units were equipped with the type, these being 41 and 85 Squadrons.

The final models of Javelin were rebuilt FAW.7s, of which 124 were converted to FAW.9 standard while forty were rebuilt as FAW.9R models. The FAW.9 incorporated slightly drooped wing leading edges, an auto pilot coupled to the radar system, jet pipes with variable area nozzles and full reheat, belly-mounted full tanks (sometimes known as Sabrinas) plus an improved radar system. The final modification was to fit an external refuelling probe on the upper starboard forward fuselage. This model became the FAW.9R and it was also fitted with modified pylons so that four 230-gallon fuel tanks could be carried for ferry flights. The FAW.9/9R was flown by eight squadrons.

Above: Gloster Javelin FAW.8 XJ130 had a very short RAF career being delivered to No. 41 Squadron in 1960. Three years later its operational life was over as the FAW.7/9 was becoming the dominant model. (AviPix)

Below: Originally built as a Javelin FAW.7 by Gloster, XH712 was originally used for Firestreak missile trials before being converted to FAW.9 standard. In this guise XH712 was flown by No. 23 Squadron, followed by a period with No. 29 Squadron. (AviPix)

When Javelin XH890 joined the RAF it was as an FAW.9R model, having been in storage for a while as an FAW.7. Operated by No. 23 Squadron and No. 29 Squadron, this fighter was badly damaged in a hard landing in Kenya. (NARA via Dennis R. Jenkins)

Did you know?

Hunter
Many will recall a Hunter flyby, that deep threnody of sound as the Avon engine sucked in its air supply. No other aircraft made that sound: it was unique.

Did you know?

Javelin
For a flight engineer working on the Javelin, the RAF beret was not only a form of headgear for day use: they used theirs to put out the odd fires caused during engine start.

4
Supersonic at Last

The silver shape slashed through the air at low level before climbing away vertically, leaving behind two towers of flame and a rumble of mighty thunder. The English Electric Lightning had arrived. Destined to be Britain's only pure supersonic jet fighter, the Lightning was designed by W. E. W. 'Teddy' Petter. Unlike previous RAF aircraft, the Lightning was the first that was able to sustain supersonic speed in level flight; it was also unusual in that it was designed from the outset as an integrated weapons system and not purely as a gun platform. To that end the airframe, flight controls, engines, armament and auto pilot were all carefully tailored to match each other. The core of the Lightning was the Ferranti AIRPASS radar, which allowed the pilot to search in front of the aircraft for possible targets. Automatic lock-on was later added to allow the radar to track the target and to guide the pilot. Once in range the system would signal the pilot when it was apposite to launch a missile. In contrast to later marques, the early tall fin Lightnings were also equipped with nose-mounted cannon just in case the further targets appeared once the paltry amount of missiles had been fired.

Following on from the F.1 came the F.1A, this featuring the capability of in-flight refuelling while the radio system was changed from VHF to UHF. The engines were also enhanced, these being the Avon 210R with a four-position reheat selector. Only two units were equipped with the type, these being 56 Squadron and 111 Squadron. The last of the tall tail Lightnings

When the Lightning entered service it was the most colourful period since the 1930s. No. 56 Squadron utilised its aircraft to form a colourful air display team. Lightning F.1A XM174/D wears this scheme. (AviPix)

Originally built as a pointed fin F.2, the aircraft later underwent rebuild to F.2A standard. In its new guise the aircraft emerged looking similar to the F.6, although the cannon were still in the nose. (AviPix)

to be manufactured was the F.2, the first of which flew in July 1961. Differences from the two earlier models included improved navigation systems, a liquid oxygen system instead of the earlier gaseous system, an offset TACAN, a steerable nose wheel and variable nozzle reheat. The only visible difference between the F.1s and the F.2 was the fitment of a small ventral intake on the spine to provide cooling for the DC standby generator. Only two units would ever fly the F.2, these being 19 and 92 Squadrons. 19 Squadron would receive their complement at Leconfield in December 1962 while the 92 Squadron deliveries would begin in April 1963. Both would retain the type as their mounts after their transfer to Germany and after many of the F.2s had been rebuilt to F.2A standard.

English Electric built the F.3 after the F.2, although by this time the company had been absorbed into the British Aircraft Corporation, BAC. This new version would be the fastest built as it had a superb power to weight ratio, the grunt being provided by a pair of Avon 301Rs. While extra speed might seem to be the ultimate, operational pilots had a different conclusion as the removal of the cannon armament reduced the fighter's firepower and its effectiveness. The primary armament was therefore the Red Top collision course missiles, these being matched to the AI23B radar. Externally, the most obvious change was the introduction of the square-topped fin, although the aircraft still retained the original small ventral tank, which reduced the available range. The first unit to receive the F.3 was 23 Squadron in August 1964, being followed by a further four squadrons.

Above: When the RAF was short of tankers the USAF would assist with Boeing KC-135s. As the USAF used boom refuelling, an adapter for probe and drogue was needed. Here a Lightning F.3 of No. 23 Squadron edges towards the trailing drogue. (NARA via Dennis R. Jenkins)

Below: In the 1970s a programme of tone-down was instituted by NATO. Buildings, vehicles, ground equipment and aircraft received a spread of mainly green. Sporting grey to go with the green is Lightning F.3 XP764 of No. 11 Squadron, based at Binbrook. (AviPix)

In the shiny days of the Lightning the unit's markings were big and bold. This Lightning F.3, XP750, was flown by No. 111 Squadron. At this time the ground equipment was overall blue-grey. (AviPix)

Following on from the F.3 came the F.3A, which drew on the earlier model but added a larger ventral tank and cranked leading edges to the wings. Later re-designated F.6 Interim, the design was finalised as the F.6, the prototype first flying in April 1964. The interim models would later be updated to full F.6 standard. While the enlarged ventral tank would increase the aircraft's range, the cambered wings also helped by reducing drag and improving range at subsonic speeds. The use of the ventral tank required two ventral fins to restore stability. The production F.6 aircraft also had plumbing for overwing wing pylons and fuel tanks to be carried; initially these were seen as range extenders, although in later years they were carried as standard. The lack of cannon was seen as a major deficiency, especially as the F.2A still retained them. The answer was to build a two-cannon gun pack into the leading section of the ventral fuel tank, with aircraft being modified from 1970 onwards. The F.3A, F.6 Interim and F.6 were operated by six squadrons.

When the Lightning entered service the RAF was indulging in colourful squadron markings, a sight not seen since the 1930s. Who can forget the red finish applied to the aircraft of 56 Squadron or their multi-aircraft displays? A similar fever gripped 74 Squadron, whose tiger badge adorned the fins of their fighters. Overall this was an unusual period in RAF history that would fade away during the NATO-inspired tone-down of the 1970s. However, this was not the end for the Lightning's colourful days as the aircraft assigned to the commanding officers of 5 and 11 Squadrons plus the Lightning Training Flight were adorned with red, black and blue fins respectively.

Above: Seen in unpainted days is Lightning F.6 XR723/L of No. 11 Squadron. By this time the cannon pack had been fitted to the forward part of the belly fuel tank. (AviPix)
Below: No. 56 Squadron was based at Akrotiri, Cyprus, prior to the civil war in 1974. XR759/P was a Lightning F.6 assigned to the squadron. At this time the only available armament for the F.6 was purely missile. (AviPix)

Currently residing at Manston in preservation is Lightning F.6 XS770/AA. As this is the squadron boss' aircraft, it sports a red fin that contrasts well against the two-tone grey of the rest of airframe. (AviPix)

Did you know?

Lightning
The Lightning could be great fuel guzzler if not managed carefully. Launching a fully armed F.6 complete with refuel probe from ground level to 40,000 feet used approximately 2,488 lbs of fuel, a quarter of the total available. Fortunately Battle Scrambles were only for Quick Reaction Alert aircraft; other Lightning drivers were asked to be a bit more careful!

Did you know?

The Lightning had a very shaky start in RAF service, being plagued by fires that normally saw the aircraft crashing, unfortunately taking the life of the pilot as well. Eventually rigorous safety checks helped contain the fire problem, thus turning the Lightning into a very capable air defence aircraft.

5
The Jet Fighter Goes To Sea

Interest in jet aircraft was not confined just to the RAF: the Royal Navy was also very interested in this emerging technology. To that end a small batch each of Gloster Meteors and de Havilland Vampires were acquired for evaluation. As these were basically land-based aircraft, both types needed modification for carrier use. The main areas that needed strengthening included the undercarriage legs and surrounding areas plus an arrestor hook was fitted to retard the airframe upon landing. Operational trials of the type took place aboard HMS *Implacable*. The trials included carrier landings and take-offs. Performance of the naval prototype Meteors proved to be favourable, including take-off performance, leading to further trials with a modified Meteor F.4 fitted with folding wings.

Although Gloster would withdraw from the naval fighter arena, de Havilland would continue developing a twin-boom fighter to replace the Sea Vampire. The follow-on aircraft developed by de Havilland was the Sea Venom, a two-seater that was crewed by a pilot and a navigator/radar operator. By the time the Sea Venom entered service all of the stability faults present in the earlier RAF aircraft had been fixed. Ten front-line units would fly the Sea Venom while a further six second-line squadrons also flew the type. The versions operated

Seen on approach to HMS *Ocean* is the prototype Sea Vampire, in the capable hands of the late Captain Eric 'Winkle' Brown RN. To fit the Vampire for naval use it required a strengthened structure and an arrestor hook. (AviPix)

The Sea Venom equipped quite a few Royal Navy squadrons. XG608 was an ECM21 model operated by No. 831 NAS. As the ECM equipment was housed in the nose of the aircraft, this required the removal of the cannon. (AviPix)

Seen aboard HMS *Eagle* is this DH Sea Venom FAW21, XG724 of No. 894 NAS. The Sea Venom not only saw combat over Egypt during the Suez Crisis of 1956, it was also used against EOKA terrorists over Cyprus in 1958. (AviPix)

Once the Sea Venom had completed is time with the front-line units, they were cascaded to second-line units for various training roles. Sea Venom FAW21 WW275 was allocated to No. 766 NAS based at Yeovilton for pilot training. (AviPix)

by the Fleet Air Arm included the FAW.20/21/22, each version featuring a slightly more powerful engine and airframe improvements. A handful each from the FAW.21 and 22 were converted for the electronic countermeasures role, the equipment requiring the removal of the cannon armament.

While de Havilland was following the path of the twin-boom fighter, Vickers Supermarine was developing and delivering the Attacker for the fighter ground attack role. Developed from the Spiteful/Seafang piston fighters, the Attacker used the wings and tailwheel undercarriage from the earlier fighters. This made carrier operation awkward as the tail-down attitude made life very difficult for the pilots, while deck landing was a nightmare.

It would be Hawker who would develop the first practical carrier fighter bomber aircraft. This was the Sea Hawk, a single-seat aircraft whose jet engine featured bifurcated intakes and exhausts. Over the years numerous models of the Sea Hawk served with the Fleet Air Arm, although near to the end of its front-line career the type was devoted completely to

The tail-down stance of the jet-powered Supermarine Attacker caused problems for pilots when landing on an aircraft carrier. FB.2 WK320 served with three front-line units until more modern equipment arrived. (AviPix)

Hawker Sea Hawk FGA.4 WV913 was allocated to No. 738 NAS at Lossiemouth. Its purpose was to introduce pilots to aerial combat. Like most Hawker aircraft the Sea Hawk was easy to fly: this made it a great ground attack aircraft. (AviPix)

the ground attack role. Thirteen front-line squadrons operated the Sea Hawk while a single reserve and eight second-line units also flew the type.

Most of the early naval jet fighters were fairly lightweight and could operate with few problems from the carriers of the day. When the heavyweight bruisers of the next generation of aircraft were looming on the horizon, the Royal Navy had already developed the angled deck and the mirror landing aid. The angled deck allowed for forward parked aircraft to be safe from landing aircraft that might be in trouble while the mirror landing aid assisted pilots in touching down on the carrier deck near the third arrestor wire.

The first heavyweight to join the Fleet Air Arm was the Supermarine Scimitar. The role of the Scimitar was air defence, conventional attack and strike. For the latter role the Scimitar was capable of carrying a nuclear weapon, although this would be a one-way trip as it was not possible to land such a weapon aboard a carrier as the safety system was very unstable.

Bearing the markings of No. 806 NAS is the preserved FGA.6 WV908. Currently awaiting a full rebuild of its engine and other systems, the Sea Hawk was once a common sight on the air show circuit. (AviPix)

Bearing the lightning flash of No. 736 NAS on the fin while based at Lossiemouth, the squadron supplied training for the remaining Scimitar squadrons. XD215 was one of the aircraft that undertook a three-ship flypast at Farnborough in September 1962. (AviPix)

While the Scimitar would serve the Royal Navy well, it did bring with it some left over baggage from the earlier Swift, although this was quickly rectified. Power for this mighty beast was delivered by a pair of Rolls-Royce Avon engines, which meant that it was capable of carrying a reasonable bomb load, underwing fuel tanks and a flight refuelling pod. The downside of this new aircraft was its unenviable habit of crashing; of the seventy-six aircraft delivered, thirty nine were lost due to crashes. Many of these crashes were due to hydraulic system problems. Added to the possibility of technical failure was the pilot's increasing workload, especially as the navigation attack system was very simple. Fortunately the vastly improved Blackburn Buccaneer, in its Mk 2 version, was on the horizon.

The final British-built fighter for the Royal Navy was the twin-boom de Havilland Sea Vixen. Based on the DH.110, this aircraft was originally designed as a fighter although in true naval fashion it soon added ground attack and aerial refuelling to its repertoire. The DH.110 prototype was lost at the Farnborough Air Show in 1952 when it broke up, killing the crew. The first version to join the Fleet Air Arm was the FAW.1, which equipped four front-line squadrons and two second-line units. Following on from the first version came the FAW.2; some were new-build aircraft while others were converted from earlier

Ground crew prepare Supermarine Scimitar F.I XD239 103/R for the 1961 Farnborough flypast courtesy of No. 800 NAS. By this time the active Scimitar fleet had been equipped with flight refuelling probes and had the capability to act as buddy tankers. (AviPix)

After their front-line career many of the surviving Scimitars went onto have a second career in the support role. One such was XD236, which was operated by the Fleet Requirements Unit at Yeovilton. (AviPix)

FAW.1 aircraft. The main visual difference was the pinion fuel tanks that extended from the booms over the wing leading edge. The FAW.2 was operated by four front-line squadrons and three second-line units.

Above: The last Sea Vixen unit to undertake active duties was No. 899 NAS, whose XJ580 is seen here. When HMS *Eagle* despatched its last Sea Vixen FAW.2 in December 1971, this closed the front-line career of this last of the twin boomers. (AviPix)

Below: A pair of Sea Vixen FAW.1s break away from each other after a flight refuelling practise. The surviving FAW.1 aircraft would later be upgraded to FAW.2 standard. (AviPix)

The only operational combat undertaken by these naval stalwarts was in the Suez Crisis in 1956, using the Sea Venom, Sea Hawk and the only naval turboprop, the Westland Wyvern torpedo attack aircraft.

This portrait of Sea Vixen FAW.2 XN696 clearly shows the major difference between it and the earlier FAW.1 – namely the extended pinion fuel tanks over the wing leading edges. Also visible is the dark-coloured hatch leading to the navigator's compartment. (AviPix)

Did you know?

Of the aircraft mentioned here, only the Hawker Sea Hawk would be sold overseas, with India, Germany and the Netherlands receiving new-build airframes. Since those days these customers have looked mainly to Russia and the United States for their equipment.

6
Canberra Ascendant

It was the arrival of the English Electric Canberra B.2 that brought Bomber Command into the jet age with a bang, over forty squadrons would be equipped with the type, at least 430 having been constructed. Having been designed by W. E. W. Petter, the prototype, VN799, had undertaken its maiden flight with Wing Commander Roland Beamont at the controls in May 1949. Likened from the outset to a jet-powered Mosquito replacement, the Canberra was designed without defensive armament, relying instead on high speed to evade any enemy.

Although the Canberra was regarded as an interim until the arrival of the V bombers, the crews trained to undertake the roles forecast for the forthcoming heavies. Originally the crew training revolved around the use of the Gee-H system that had been developed during the Second World War and which was the primary blind bombing aid. Over half the missions flown by the Canberra crews would end with a Gee-H attack. However, this system proved less than reliable as it could be jammed by a basic electronic jamming system. This was not the main defect as the system had serious reliability issues; not only did the aircraft receivers fail at inconsiderate moments, the ground stations also failed on occasion. Given the possibility of system failure, it would come as no surprise to find the Canberra crews relying more on visual bombing courtesy of the on-board optical bomb sight.

Seen taxiing in at Tengah is this Canberra B.15, WT209 of No. 45 Squadron. Of note is the large squadron badge on the fin. Unfortunately this aircraft was written off after undercarriage problems resulted in a belly landing. (AviPix)

Even so, when working within these confines the Canberras could easily outfly the available British fighters, this giving rise to great concern to those charged with Britain's air defence. While the aircraft manufacturers strove to create fighters capable of intercepting incoming bombers, there were also developments happening in the world of bomber defence. The first such system applied to the Canberra, and also the Valiant, was the Orange Putter, an active tail warning radar. Fitted in the tail cone, this unit was designed to detect incoming fighters preparing to undertake a tail-on attack.

Overall, the British crews continued their normal training; however, there were attempts to improve the defensive systems fitted to the aircraft. While Orange Putter had fallen out of favour, the increasing capability of Warsaw Pact defensive systems meant that other methods had to be found to protect the bombers and to improve their blind bombing capability. It was the need for a self-contained blind bombing system that was the real need as the Gee-H system was increasingly vulnerable to jamming. The answer would be the Blue Shadow sideways-looking airborne radar. Initial trials originally gave a good report of the system; however, continued in-service use revealed that it required extensive preparation by the crews before an operation was undertaken. The conclusion by Bomber Command was that Blue Shadow should be used only by aircraft dedicated to target marking while the remaining Canberras would revert to their normal visual bombing practise.

Obviously, the normal high-speed visual attack run was not a viable option when nuclear weapons became part of the Canberra inventory. The answer would be to adopt the American Low Altitude Bombing System, LABS, this having been adopted by the USAF in 1954. Instead of buying the already available Honeywell developed system, it was decided that the British would develop their own. In typical British fashion there were the inevitable delays, thus a number of Honeywell systems were purchased as a stopgap. LABS did have its downside: one of its lesser faults was an occasional bomb-release failure, although the bomb did drop out after the pull-out, an embarrassment to all concerned.

During 1954, following the build-up of Soviet forces in Eastern Europe, it was decided to establish a Canberra Wing at Gütersloh in Germany to carry out night intruder duties; as development of a dedicated intruder version was some way off, it was decided that existing B.6 airframes would be modified to carry a gun pack and have pylons fitted to enable the carriage of rocket launchers or bombs. Twenty-two of these interim aircraft, designated Canberra B(I)6, were converted and issued to 213 Squadron.

While the intruder version of the B.6 was a capable machine, it was obvious that a more dedicated aircraft was needed. The answer was a revamped aircraft with a redesigned nose; however, the chance was missed to create a tandem two-seat nose as fitted to the American-built Canberras. The first of the new aircraft, designated as B(I)8s, flew for the first time in July 1954, with the first deliveries to 88 Squadron in mid-1956. These aircraft featured a revised fighter-type cockpit, offset to port to improve the visibility for the pilot. The navigator's position was also moved forward of the pilot into the nose, although he did not have an ejection seat. From January 1958, the B(I)8 squadrons were committed to the low-altitude tactical bombing role. This involved a high-speed, low-level approach to the target area, followed by a sharp pull up into a loop, in the course of which a nuclear store was released.

Above: Wearing a large fin badge is Canberra B(I)6 WT316 of No. 213 Squadron. Based at Bruggen, the unit disbanded in 1969 when further B(I)8s became available. During its service time eight B(I)6s were lost from the nineteen delivered. (AviPix)

Below: Originally built as a Canberra B.2, WH957 was later rebuilt as an E.15 for electronic checking purposes, being operated by No. 98 Squadron based at Cottesmore and remaining active until 1976. (AviPix)

Above: This formation represents some of the Canberra strike force available to RAFG. To the front is a Canberra B(I)8 of No. 16 Squadron complete with under-belly gunpack. The next two machines are Canberra B(I)6s of No. 213 Squadron. (AviPix)

Below: Providing much-needed reconnaissance support were the Canberra PR.7s of No. 13 Squadron that spent time at Luqa, Malta, before returning home to Wyton. WT821 is seen at Wyton awaiting its crew. This airframe is on display at Bassingbourn. (AviPix)

The Canberra PR.9 was the final version to enter RAF service and remained the only strategic reconnaissance aircraft available once the Victor SR.2 had been retired. XH175 served with No. 39 Squadron. This unit remained active until 2006. (AviPix)

Did you know?

Having designed the Canberra and the Lightning for English Electric, W. E. W. Petter moved to Folland, where he led the team developing the Midge and Gnat fighters.

Did you know?

The Canberra was the only British aircraft to penetrate the American market, emerging as the Martin B-57, complete with tandem cockpits, rotating bomb door and cannon in the wings.

7
V Bombers to the Fore

In the 1950s, the RAF was considered to be the main carrier for any home-brewed nuclear weapons; however, the only aircraft available was the Avro Lincoln, already well past its sell-by date. To that end development requests were sent to various aircraft manufacturers, of which those from Avro, Handley Page and Vickers were chosen for further development.

The Vickers Valiant was a four-engined high-winged monoplane powered by Rolls-Royce Avon engines that also provided pneumatic and electrical power to the aircraft systems. While seen as a simple aircraft the Valiant featured some interesting innovations; not only were the flaps and undercarriage electrically driven, the main gear units were tandem in design, although each wheel was mounted on a separate undercarriage leg. The crew were housed in a pressurised cabin and consisted of two pilots, two navigators and a signaller, later upgraded to an air electronics operator. Various versions of the Valiant were delivered; these including the B.1, a pure bomber variant, and the B(PR), a bomber/photo reconnaissance aircraft that could accommodate a removable crate in the bomb bay. Also delivered was the B(PR)K.1, a bomber/photo reconnaissance/ tanker aircraft, plus the B(K).1, a bomber/ tanker aircraft. Both tanker variants carried a removable tanker system in the bomb bay, this featuring fuel tanks and a hose/drogue aerial refuelling system.

In 1960 the Lockheed U-2 flown by Gary Powers was shot down over Russia; this revealed that the SAM threat was greater than first realised, which caused the V-Force to train for

Photographed at Weybridge is Vickers Valiant B.1 WZ367, resplendent in low-level colours. The bomber had been flown by Nos 138, 49 and 148 Squadrons before moving to Weybridge to develop a repair scheme for the rear spar cracking problem. (AviPix)

low-level attack. Unfortunately, low-level operations proved too much for the Valiant and on 6 August 1964 there was a failure of a rear spar in an aircraft from Gaydon. The aircraft landed safely back at base, but without a flap due to damage in the rear of one wing. Inspection of the entire fleet showed that the wing spars were suffering from fatigue due to low-level turbulence. Therefore, in early 1965 the Wilson government decided that the expense of the repairs could not be justified and the fleet was permanently grounded in January 1965.

The aircraft that would survive the longest in the bombing role was the Avro Vulcan. Designed under the guidance of Roy Chadwick – designer of the Lancaster of the Second World War – the initial design was a pure delta that would make one flight only. Eventually common sense prevailed and the Vulcan shape recognised by many came into being. The first prototype, VX770, undertook its maiden flight in August 1952, while the second prototype, VX777, would join the flight test programme in September 1953.

Early on in the Vulcan's career a major problem reared its head: in level flight at high speed, the aircraft showed a tendency to pitch up. Much effort was expended on curing this fault. The answer was a cranked and kinked wing leading edge plus auto stabilisers that would reduce the pitch problem; most of the fleet would either have this modification embodied or would be delivered with it as standard. The Vulcan B.1 was intended to carry either the Yellow Sun or Red Beard free-fall nuclear weapon that would be dropped from high altitude; to that end they were finished in gloss white anti-flash paint. Missing in the early B.1 was a dedicated ECM installation; however, this was catered for by installing the ECM equipment in the bomb bay, although to support this a turbo generator was installed to cover the electrical requirements. Obviously when conventional bombs were loaded the ECM equipment had to be off-loaded to make room.

Still sporting an overall white finish is Valiant BK.1 XD816, wearing the fin badge of No. 214 Squadron. During the Suez Crisis in 1956 this aircraft, among others, undertook bombing missions over Egypt while part of No. 148 Squadron. (AviPix)

Three Avro Vulcan B.1s in formation is a rare occurrence. These aircraft are all assigned to the Waddington Wing, as revealed by the fin badge. All three feature the cranked leading edge fitted to counter a tendency to pitch up in level flight. (AviPix)

Only thirty-five Vulcan B.1s would be built as this version was seen as an interim model; the B.2 that would emerge in August 1958 was a far more advanced machine. Powerplants were more powerful Olympus 200 series engines in place of the earlier Olympus 100 engines. The airframe also underwent changes: the wings had their span extended while the leading edge was also cranked as per the earlier model. The fuselage also underwent some changes; the ECM equipment was installed in a purposely designed tail cone while a refuelling probe was installed in the nose. Both of these modifications were embodied in the earlier B.1s, these being re-designated B.1A after conversion. Initially the Vulcan B.2s were delivered in anti-flash white finish with the correct pale coloured national markings.

Originally the B.2s were slated to carry the same nuclear weapons as the B.1s; however, the improvements in Soviet air defences meant that the Vulcan fleet was more vulnerable and therefore another means of delivery was needed. The answer would be the Blue Steel stand-off weapon. The project was led by Avro, whose sub-contractors would provide a very capable inertial navigation system while the powerplant was the Bristol-designed Stentor engine whose fuel was the highly volatile hydrogen peroxide. After numerous trials at home and Australia the first weapons were issued to 617 Squadron in September 1962, although these weapons were designated for national emergency use only until the fully developed version was available. When the decision was taken to swap the Vulcan to the low-level role in 1964, the aircraft were repainted in upper surface camouflage while the Blue Steel delivery tactics were altered to suit.

The final member of the V Bomber triumvirate to join the RAF would be the Handley Page Victor. Beaten into the air by the Vulcan prototype that flew in August 1952, those

Possibly one of the cleanest shots ever of a Vulcan B.2 is this one of a No. 617 Squadron aircraft, complete with Blue Steel training round under the belly. (NARA via Dennis R. Jenkins)

When the Blue Steel started to get old, the intended replacement was the Douglas Skybolt ICBM. Vulcan B.2 XH537 was assigned to act as the trials aircraft. Initially the missile suffered numerous launch and flight problems. (NARA via Dennis R. Jenkins)

building the Victor had to wait until Christmas Eve to get their contender into the skies. Although the Victor prototypes performed within design specifications, there were a few design miscalculations that eventually led to the loss of WB771 on 14 July 1954, when the tailplane detached while making a low-level pass over the runway at Cranfield.

Production B.1 Victors were powered by Armstrong Siddeley Sapphire engines and were originally configured to deliver the Blue Danube nuclear weapon, later re-equipping with the more powerful Yellow Sun weapon when it became available; later the Red Beard tactical nuclear weapon was added to the inventory when it became available. A total of twenty-four were later upgraded to B.1A standard by the addition of Red Steer tail warning radar in an enlarged tailcone and a suite of ECM jammers between 1958 and 1960.

The RAF later recognised a requirement for a higher ceiling for its bombers, and a number of proposals were considered for improved Victors to meet this demand. Handley Page proposed the interim Phase 2A Victor powered by the Conway engine, with the airframe having minimal modifications. In contrast to the B.1, the B.2 featured distinctive retractable elephant ear intakes on the rear fuselage, forward of the fin, that fed ram air to turbine-driven alternators. In the event of a high-altitude flameout or other engine problem that caused the loss of electrical or hydraulic power, the RAT scoops would open and provide sufficient electrical power to work the flight controls until the main engines could be relit. The right wing root also incorporated an Artouste airborne auxiliary power plant, AAPP. This small engine could provide high-pressure air for engine starting, electrical power on the ground, or in the air as an emergency backup in the event of main engine failure. The aircraft also featured a fin extension at the base that containing the ECM cooling equipment. The first prototype Victor B.2 undertook its maiden flight in February 1959. The aircraft had flown 100 hours quite safely when, on 20 August 1959, while undertaking high-altitude engine tests for the Aeroplane and Armament Experimental Establishment, it disappeared from radar screens, crashing into the sea off the coast of Pembrokeshire.

A total of twenty-one B.2 aircraft were upgraded to B.2 Blue Steel standard with Conway engines of increased thrust. The wings were modified to incorporate two pods or Küchemann carrots, which were anti-shock bodies that reduced wave drag at transonic speeds and housed

Originally ordered for the SAAF, these three Handley Page Victors B.1s were delivered to the RAF and No. 15 Squadron. Finished in anti-flash white overall, the effect was spoiled by the use of standard colour national markings and underwing serials. (AviPix)

Delivered as a Victor B.2, complete with its capability to carry thirty-five 1,000 lb bombs, XL231 was delivered to No. 139 Squadron. Converted to carry the Blue Steel missile in 1964, the aircraft was assigned to the Wittering Wing. (AviPix)

Although available to the RAF from 1963, Victor SR.2 XL161 was converted for the strategic reconnaissance role and later sampling equipment was added to the front of the underwing tanks as shown here. (AviPix)

the chaff dispensers. With the move to low-level penetration attack profiles, the Victors were fitted with refuelling probes above the cockpit, large underwing fuel tanks plus a coat of two-tone camouflage finish in place of the original anti-flash white.

The loss of the Valiant in the air tanker role left a major gap in British air defences. The solution was to convert the by now redundant Victor B.1 bombers into K.1 tankers. These equipped three squadrons and a small conversion flight at Marham. With the Victor tankers now available it was possible for the Lightnings to intercept incoming Russian snoopers further out into the North Sea. While the K.1s gave sterling service it was obvious that their working lives would be short. The answer was to initially take the Victor B.2 bombers that had lost their purpose once Blue Steel had been retired in 1970 and convert them into tankers. By this time Handley Page had gone out of business so the task of creating the K.2 tankers was taken on by Hawker Siddeley. Latecomers to the conversion line would be the few remaining Victor SR.2s that were still providing a measure of strategic reconnaissance at Wyton. Eventually these few machines were also converted into tankers.

In 1970 the Vulcans were deployed at Scampton and Waddington with a pair of squadrons based at Akrotiri in Cyprus. The civil war in Cyprus during late 1974 and early 1975 saw the bomber squadrons being withdrawn to Britain, both of the home stations received a squadron. In April 1975 Strike Command decided that creating semi-autonomous squadrons at both stations would create a sense of identity and better morale. Thus at Scampton 35 and 617 Squadrons plus 230 OCU came into existence, later to be joined by 27 Squadron for reconnaissance duties. Over at Waddington 9, 44, 50 and 101 Squadrons became the resident units.

By 1982 the Vulcan force was in decline; all of the Scampton units had been disbanded while at Waddington only 9 Squadron had relinquished its bombers. This left 44, 50 and 101 Squadrons as the only Vulcan operators. Many of the withdrawn Waddington Vulcans had been sent to St Athan for disposal and it was here that a delegation from the Argentine Air Force arrived to discuss the possibility of purchasing some of the withdrawn aircraft plus spares and support.

This transaction was never completed, fortunately, as Argentina decided to invade the Falkland Islands in April. Had they delayed by a month or so they might have got away with

Above: Seen at Waddington in the mid-1970s is Vulcan B.2 XM648 of No. 101 Squadron. XM648 replaced XM575 as the 101 Squadron scramble aircraft during the Queen's Silver Jubilee in 1977 as XM575 had blown an engine starter during a practise. (AviPix)

Below: Seen here at Scampton, sporting the fin badge of No. 27 Squadron in its reconnaissance days, XH563 had spent much of its previous career as a bomber plus a short spell as a Skybolt trials aircraft. Fortunately the nose survives in Yorkshire. (AviPix)

it as the Royal Navy was about to suffer severe cutbacks, while the Vulcans would have completely disappeared. Argentina also though that Britain would fail to respond; however, both countries had leaders who were in trouble.

While the Royal Navy would put together a task force centred around the carriers HMS *Hermes* and HMS *Invincible*, the RAF was sending assets to Ascension Island that included much of the Victor tanker fleet plus a handful of Vulcans. The bombers had been fitted with bespoke underwing pylons and GPS and the inflight refuelling system had been restored to working order. The Vulcan missions to the Falklands were designated as Operation Black Buck and the first mission was launched against Port Stanley airfield on 30 April. Using a rotating fleet of Victor tankers the bomber made it to the target before returning to Ascension with another fleet of Victor tankers to bring them home. Two other airfield attacks were made, both successfully, while a further two targeted the air defence radars. While the bomb runs over the airfield seemed to have inflicted much physical damage, the attacks also sent two messages: that a 1,000 lb bomb will have a serious effect on those on the other end, and that bombers reaching the Falklands meant Buenos Aires was within reach.

With the surrender of the Argentine forces in June 1982 the rundown of the Vulcan force continued until a handful remained as single point tankers until the VC10 tankers were ready. As for the Victors, they continued in service until 1993, although the fleet was slowly shrinking as fatigue lives were consumed. Even so, the Victors had one last hurrah undertaking the vital tanking role during Operation Desert Storm in 1991.

Did you know?

The first batch of Vulcan B.2s utilised the main fuselage sections from the last B.1 order. Unlike the main production machines, these had the smaller intakes of the B.1s as in XH558, recently grounded, and were never fitted with the TFR pod in the nose.

Vulcan
'This is the Bomber Controller – Readiness State 05.' Chaos, coffee cups, fags and cards whirl into the air during the mad scramble for the door. Run like hell to the bomber. Power set on, covers removed, back chocks gone, front chocks loosened. Crew buses arrive, crew chief opens door, AEO signals 28 volts on. Power set comes on line. Crew chief on headset, raises two fingers for readiness two. The fandango begins. Scream of rapids, deep rumble reverberates. 200 volt cable away, 28 cable away. Go to front chocks, remove on signal, leg it to hide behind the plinth. Crew chief waves at crew and joins us. Engines at 80 per cent, the Vulcan clears the slot. Up to full power on the turn and down the runway. All four gone in under two minutes. Silence and then the birds begin to sing.

8
The Last British Bomber

In the 1950s, the Royal Navy found itself needing to respond to the threat posed by the rapid expansion of the Soviet Navy. Prominent among Soviet naval developments were the Sverdlov class cruisers, these being fast and well-armed. This made them a serious threat to merchant shipping in the Atlantic. To counter this the Royal Navy decided to introduce a specialised strike aircraft that could employ conventional or nuclear weapons. Operating from the fleet carriers and attacking at high speed and low level, it would offer a solution to the Sverdlov cruisers.

To get the ball rolling, a detailed specification was issued that requested a two-seat aircraft with folding wings for carrier stowage. The new strike aircraft had to be capable of flying at high speed at low level with a load of conventional bombs or the Red Beard free-fall nuclear weapon. Based on this requirement, the Ministry of Supply issued a specification in August 1952. Blackburn's design by Roy Boot won the tender in July 1955. The first prototype made its maiden flight from RAE Bedford in April 1958.

What was rolled out of the door at Brough was a mid-winged aircraft with a crew of two seated in tandem. The outer wing sections took up most of the wingspan and were hydraulically folding and locking. On the trailing edge of the wings were a pair of small flaps on the inner wing sections while the whole outer wing panels had a single movable surface that could act as ailerons, though during take-off and landing they could be drooped to use as flaps retaining some roll control. To keep the aircraft size to within the limits of British aircraft carriers, the Buccaneer was fitted with a boundary layer control system, which blew high pressure air over the wings, flaps and tailplane. Weapons could be carried in the bomb bay – this being unique in having a rotating door to mount the bombs on. Four pylon positions were available under the wings, while unique slipper fuel tanks were installed under the inner wing sections, which also housed the undercarriage, engines and jet pipes.

The first production Buccaneer S.1 entered squadron service with the Fleet Air Arm in January 1963. It was powered by a pair of de Havilland Gyron Junior turbojets that left the aircraft underpowered and as a consequence it could not be launched fully laden with

The first version of the Buccaneer to enter Fleet Air Arm service was the S.1. No. 800 Squadron would fly XN970 107/E from HMS *Eagle*. This was one of the aircraft lost due to engine problems. (AviPix)

fuel and weapons. A temporary solution to this problem was the buddy refuelling system. The Buccaneer launched with a full load of weapons and minimal fuel, joining up with a Supermarine Scimitar for refuelling. The lack of power meant that the loss of an engine during take-off or landing at full load, when the aircraft was heavily dependent on its boundary layer control system, could be catastrophic.

The long-term solution to the underpowered S.1 was the development of the Buccaneer S.2, this being fitted with the Rolls-Royce Spey engine, which provided more thrust. The engine nacelles had to be enlarged to accommodate the Spey and the wing required modification as a result. Hawker Siddeley announced the production order for the S.2 in January 1962, with all Fleet Air Arm squadrons converting by the end of 1966.

Some Fleet Air Arm Buccaneers were modified to carry the Martel anti-ship missile, these being later re-designated S.2D. The RAF aircraft were also given various upgrades that included an ECM pod, chaff/flare dispensers and Sidewinder missile capability. In 1979, the RAF obtained the American Pave Spike laser designator pod for Paveway II guided bombs, allowing the Buccaneer to act as a target designator for other Buccaneers, Jaguars, and others.

The Buccaneer entered service with the Fleet Air Arm in July 1962 when 801 Naval Air Squadron (NAS) was commissioned at Lossiemouth. In addition to conventional ordnance, the Buccaneer was approved for nuclear weapons delivery in 1965. Weapons deployed included Red Beard, this being replaced later by WE.177 bombs carried internally on the rotating bomb bay door. Two Fleet Air Arm operational squadrons and a training unit were equipped with the Buccaneer S.1. As the Buccaneer S.1's Gyron Junior engines were not powerful enough, this led to the type's career coming to an abrupt end in December 1970. During this month two aircraft were lost due to engine problems; subsequent inspections concluded that the Gyron Junior engine was no longer safe for combat operations and all surviving S.1s were grounded permanently.

By April 1965 intensive trials of the new Buccaneer S.2 had begun, with the type entering operational service later that year. The improved S.2 proved its value when it became the first FAA aircraft to make a non-stop, unrefuelled crossing of the Atlantic Ocean. In 1972 Buccaneers of 809 NAS operating from HMS *Ark Royal* took part in a 1,500-mile mission to show a military presence over British Honduras, now Belize, shortly before its independence, to deter a possible Guatemalan invasion in pursuit of their territorial claims over the country. The Buccaneer left Fleet Air Arm service with the decommissioning in 1978 of HMS *Ark Royal*, the last navy fleet carrier. The Royal Navy would later replace the naval strike capability of the Buccaneer with the smaller V/STOL capable British Aerospace Sea Harriers that were operated from the Invincible class aircraft carriers.

Once the F-111K had been cancelled in early 1968, the RAF was forced to look at the Buccaneer. The first RAF unit to receive the Buccaneer was 12 Squadron at Honington in October 1969. Honington was to remain a key station for the type as 15 Squadron equipped with the Buccaneer the following year, before moving to Laarbruch in 1971 while the RAF Buccaneer conversion unit, 237 OCU, formed at Honington in March 1971. Ex-navy aircraft equipped 16 Squadron, joining 15 Squadron at Laarbruch, while in Britain 208 Squadron equipped with the type at Honington. During the 1970s the five operational units consisted of three squadrons, 15, 16 and 208 Squadrons, plus 237 OCU, all assigned to Supreme Allied Commander Europe (SACEUR) for land strike duties in support of land forces opposing Warsaw Pact land forces on the Continent, while 12 Squadron was assigned to SACLANT for maritime strike duties.

The Buccaneer S.2 was a vast improvement over the earlier S.1 courtesy of the Spey engines. XT280 is seen here at Lossiemouth awaiting a return to No. 809 NAS and HMS *Ark Royal*. The Royal Navy utilised the Buccaneer until 1978. (AviPix)

Buccaneer XV165, seen here sporting the fox badge of No. 12 Squadron, had served with the Royal Navy before transfer. After many years with the squadron it spent its last years with 237 OCU. The nose is currently on display at Farnborough. (AviPix)

Buccaneer S.2B XW537 spent much of its ten years of service life in Germany. Initially operated by XV Squadron, it later transferred to No. 16 Squadron, also at Laarbruch. XW537 was lost in a crash in 1981 on approach to Wattisham. (AviPix)

Opportunities for Buccaneer squadrons to engage in realistic training were limited so when the Americans began their Red Flag military exercises at Nellis Air Force Base in 1975 the RAF expressed interest. The first Red Flag in which RAF aircraft were involved was in 1977, with ten Buccaneers and two Avro Vulcan bombers participating. The Buccaneer proved an impressive bomber with its fast low-level attacks that were highly accurate despite the lack of terrain-following radar and other modern avionics. They were able to penetrate adversary defences, being credited with kills against defending fighters using AIM-9 Sidewinder missile simulators.

During the 1980 Red Flag exercise one of the participating Buccaneers lost a wing in flight due to a fatigue-induced crack in the inner wing spectacle and crashed, killing the crew. The entire RAF Buccaneer fleet was grounded in February 1980; subsequent investigation discovered serious metal fatigue problems to be present on numerous aircraft. A total of sixty aircraft were rated as worth repairing; however, as new inner ring spars were impossible to manufacture, it was decided to inspect all of the available aircraft, from which the best would be repaired if possible by replacement of the inner wing sections, while others could have the damage blended out. Once the initial repairs and inspections had been completed, some form of deterrent was quickly made available. The long-term solution of replacing the inner wing sections would result in a collection of fully stripped Buccaneers awaiting scrapping while the remainder returned to service. Changes to the Buccaneer force followed with 216 Squadron disappearing so fast it barely made a mark. Nos 15 and 16 Squadrons were on their way to the Panavia Tornado while 12 and 208 Squadrons were switched to the maritime role moving to Lossiemouth in concert with the OCU.

The Buccaneer would take part in combat operations during Desert Storm, the combat phase of the 1991 Gulf War. Following a quick decision to deploy, the first batch of six aircraft were readied to depart in under 72 hours, including the adoption of desert camouflage and additional equipment, departing from Lossiemouth for the Middle East theatre early in January 1991. In theatre it became common for each attack formation to comprise four Tornados and two Buccaneers; each Buccaneer carried a single laser designator pod and acted as backup to the other in the event of an equipment malfunction. The Buccaneers flew

When XW866 'Y' was transferred from the RN it had already been made compatible with the Martel missile. Seen here on an early Red Flag exercise in 1979, the aircraft would be withdrawn for use in the inner wing donor programme. (AviPix)

In 1972 Buccaneer S.2B XW540 was allocated to No. 15 Squadron at Laarbruch. However, with the Panavia Tornado starting to replace the Buccaneer it was decided to form another unit at Honington, this being No. 216 Squadron. (AviPix)

After service aboard both HMS *Eagle* and HMS *Ark Royal* Buccaneer S.2 XV353 was transferred to the RAF. Serving with Nos 12 and 208 Squadrons respectively, the Buccaneer remained active until withdrawn from use in 1993. (AviPix)

218 missions during the Gulf War, in which they designated targets for other aircraft and dropped forty-eight laser-guided bombs.

It had originally been planned for the Buccaneer to remain in service until the end of the 1990s, having been extensively modernised up to 1989; the end of the Cold War stimulated major changes in British defence policy, many aircraft being deemed surplus to requirements. It was decided that a number of Panavia Tornado GR1s would be modified for compatibility with the Sea Eagle missile and take over the RAF's maritime strike mission, and the Buccaneer would be retired early. The last Buccaneers were withdrawn in March 1994 when 208 Squadron disbanded.

Seen here in flight is Buccaneer S.2B XV332, which sports the finish applied for deployment during Operation Granby. Although it carries the artwork *Dirty Harriet* on the nose, the lack of fin code letter confirms its status as the backup aircraft. (AviPix)

Did you know?

Throughout its career, the Buccaneer was known as the banana or nana jet. This was based on the design entry designation file, headed BANA, which stood for Blackburn Aircraft Naval Aircraft.

9
Going Vertical

Strike Command would gain one of the most innovative aircraft in the world during 1969. This was the Hawker Siddeley Harrier, which had begun life as the Hawker P.1127. Once the design had been fully detailed, NATO military staffs prepared a design requirement for a lightweight V/STOL (Vertical/Short Take-Off and Landing) fighter based on the P.1127 design.

Construction of the first P.1127 began using private funding in 1959, although the Ministry of Aviation later gave backing for the construction of two prototype aircraft. Construction continued apace with first hover trials taking place during October 1960, while the first conventional flight was undertaken in March 1961. Kingston further developed the P.1127 design, the interested parties being Britain, the United States and West Germany. The result was an order for nine improved models known as the Kestrel, these being destined for the Tripartite Evaluation Squadron based at West Raynham.

At the core of the Harrier was the Pegasus engine that vented through four nozzles, two each side of the fuselage. All four nozzles were driven by air drawn from the compressor; this removed the need for hydraulic and electrical power supplies, all of which reduced the weight of the aircraft. Great care was also taken in ensuring that the Harrier could operate safely from unprepared surfaces and minimal prepared surfaces without causing damage to the airframe.

From the pilot's point of view his primary avionics system was the Ferranti inertial nav/ attack system. The data was supplied to the pilot via a Head-Up Display (HUD) system, this being capable of displaying navigation data, weapon aiming plus night and VTOL flying. The core of this system was the moving map display.

Of course, the primary role of the Harrier was to pop out of concealment and let loose its weaponry at its designated targets. This was only possible due to the aircraft's design and its ability to operate from semi- or unprepared strips. During a war scenario the Harrier force could be widely dispersed in hides that, with careful concealment, were virtually undetectable, unlike conventional aircraft that required the full gamut of support facilities in order to be operable. To that end the Harrier was equipped with a pair of pods under the fuselage that were home to a pair of 30 mm cannon. Between the pods was the centreline pylon that could carry either weaponry or a reconnaissance pod. Other weaponry could be carried on the four underwing pylons, with the inner pylons being plumbed for the carriage of fuel tanks.

The RAF would originally order sixty airframes, comprising fifty single-seat aircraft plus ten two-seat conversion airframes, although the final total would reach 131 airframes. The second contract would include further GR.1 airframes plus twenty-four GR.3s and seventeen extra two-seaters. The GR.1A featured an uprated Pegasus and after converting the remaining original GR.1s, a total of fifty-eight aircraft were available. In order to improve the aircraft's capabilities, the Harrier was updated to the GR.3, this having the Ferranti LRMTS (Laser Rangefinder and Marked Target Seeker) in the nose. As the name implies, the aircraft's system calculates the closure rate and distance of a specified spot via the laser detector and detects the illuminated target. Although this improved the aircraft's combat options, it still relied upon the target being illuminated by an external source.

Four units were equipped with the early Harriers, these being 1, 3, 4 and 20 Squadrons, although the latter three were based in Germany. Initially training was carried out by the Harrier Conversion Unit based at Wittering that had formed in January 1969, although this was later re-designated as 233 OCU.

The only Harrier unit that would be based in Britain would be 1 Squadron, based at Wittering, where it would become part of Air Support Command. Prior to equipping with the Harrier the squadron had flown the Hunter. The Harrier GR.1 was formally released for service use in April 1969 and shortly afterwards would participate in the Daily Mail Trans-Atlantic Air Race organised to commemorate the fiftieth anniversary of Flt Lts Alcock and Brown's first non-stop flight across the Atlantic. On 5 May, Sqn Ldr Tom Lecky-Thompson took off vertically in XV741 from St Pancras railway station and, utilising in-flight refuelling, landed vertically in New York's Bristol Basin. The race was from the top of the London Post Office Tower to the top of the Empire State Building; the winning flight time was 6 hours 11 minutes.

The early days of the Harrier fleet sees this GR.1 of No. 1 Squadron practising operating out of a rubb and on metal matting in an effort to simulate field operations. The real thing was far more gritty and tiring. (AviPix)

Germany and Gutersloh was home for the Harrier force squadrons, three of which were based there. GR.1 XV797/S was on the strength of No. 20 Squadron when photographed. Later converted to GR.3 configuration, it was then issued to No. 4 Squadron. (AviPix)

Hawker Siddeley Harrier GR.1 XW765/D was assigned to No. 20 Squadron. After conversion to GR.3 standard it was flown by No. 3 Squadron, with whom it was serving when it suffered a bird strike over North Wales and crashed. (AviPix)

Carrying a full fin version of the nose bars is Harrier GR.3 XZ969/D of No. 4 Squadron from Wildenrath. After completion of its service the Harrier was used as a training airframe by the Royal Navy before being dumped at Predannack. (AviPix)

In 1975 No. 1 Squadron despatched six Harriers to the British colony of Belize in Central America as neighbouring Guatemala had yet again been threatening another incursion across the border, although this time the threat was real as troops and equipment were seen gathering on the border. After five months of flying armed along the border, the Harriers returned home as the Guatemalan forces had withdrawn back to their barracks. The respite was short, however, as by June 1977 the Guatemalans were threatening to invade again, thus a more permanent force was established, designated 1417 Flight and based at Ladyville airport.

Given the British determination to protect Belize, the Guatemalans decided that diplomacy might be a better course. The first step was taken in 1991 when Guatemala recognised that the people of Belize should determine their own future. This was followed in 1992 when the President of Guatemala recognised the independence of Belize and established diplomatic relations between both countries. During 1993, with the peace in the area seemingly settled, it was decided to withdraw 1417 Flight, this marking the end of the Harrier GR.3 in RAF service as the more advanced GR.5 was in the process of being delivered.

The removal of HMS *Ark Royal* left the Royal Navy in a quandary; for the first time in many years there were no carriers available for fleet defence, although a solution was on the horizon. The first of the through deck cruisers – in essence mini aircraft carriers – had been launched in 1973, joining the fleet in 1980. Two sister ships were also built, these being *Illustrious*, commissioned 1982, and *Ark Royal*, commissioned 1985. Obviously these fine vessels were useless without aircraft and a V/STOL solution was needed. As the RAF Harrier had shown great worth, Hawker Siddeley were contracted to develop a navalised version for the Fleet Air Arm. Basing the Shar, as it became known, on the RAF GR.3, the major changes involved the nose section, where the canopy was raised to increase all-round visibility while the nose was extended to house the Blue Fox radar.

Initial deliveries were made to Yeovilton to equip 899 NAS, the shore-based headquarters and training unit, while the first sea-going unit was 800 NAS, followed soon afterwards by 801 NAS, all being available from 1981. A total of fifty-seven FRS.1 aircraft were delivered for naval use.

The Falklands War would bring the Sea Harrier into sharp focus as they would be the only fighters able to deploy close to the islands. Twenty-eight were split between HMS *Invincible* and the commando carrier HMS *Hermes*; both now sported the bow ski ramps that allowed a heavily loaded aircraft to get airborne at speed over a short distance. Not only did the Shar

Sporting the colourful markings of No. 800 NAS, this early delivery Sea Harrier FRS.1 is XZ458, assigned to the light carrier HMS *Invincible*. This Sea Harrier would not reach the FA.2 conversion programme as it crashed in December 1984. (AviPix)

Yet another early Sea Harrier that was lost in a crash, only this time it was over the Falkland Islands. Seen in happier days, XZ452 101/VL was allocated to No. 899 NAS, which acted as the shore-based headquarters unit at Yeovilton. (AviPix)

Sitting on the launch ramp of HMS *Hermes* is this unidentified Sea Harrier FRS.1, showing the wear and tear of combat operations over the Falkland Islands. Later this airframe would go through the FA.2 conversion programme. (AviPix)

The Sea Harrier FA.2 was a total rebuild of the original airframes, plus there were some new builds. One of the new builds was ZH798/002, seen here launching from HMS *Invincible*. (NARA via Dennis R. Jenkins)

exceed all expectations during this conflict, their ability to out-manoeuvre enemy aircraft ensured that none were shot down.

After the Falklands War it was decided to upgrade the remaining FRS.1 machines to the improved FA.2. Not only were the surviving aircraft reworked, but a new-build batch was added to replace those lost through accidents. The FA.2 featured a new radar, the Blue Vixen, and a fuselage that had been increased in length, this allowing for an improved equipment fit and improved stability. The FA.2 deliveries began in 1993, with this version remaining in front-line use until controversially withdrawn in 2006.

Did you know?

Prior to joint operation to fly Harriers by the RAF and the Royal Navy from the Invincible class carriers, some cross-decking by the RAF was carried out. There were numerous complaints that covered the need to learn 'boaty speak' and the fact that the airfield kept bouncing up and down.

10

The Great White Hope

In 1957 the Minister of Defence, Duncan Sandys, issued a defence white paper that would see a massive reorganisation of Britain's armed forces. Two aviation ideas would grab the headlines: that all air defence, both offensive and defensive, could be covered by the use of missiles, while only flown projects would be allowed to continue. A slight modification to that statement was that the major manufacturing companies should be concentrated into two major groups to bid on contracts. Much of this had already happened, as Hawker Aircraft already included Avro and Gloster, while the other group would be centred around a merger of English Electric and Vickers, leading to the formation of the British Aircraft Corporation. The only company not to join either group was Handley Page whose boss, Sir Frederick Handley Page, reckoned that his company could go it alone.

The forcing together of English Electric and the Vickers group into BAC would see both merging to create the next strike aircraft for the RAF. The intended aircraft due for replacement was the Canberra, which was getting long in the tooth and very vulnerable to Soviet air defences. Causing consternation among the ranks of the RAF was the emergence of the Royal Navy and its Buccaneer project; this was already being touted as a Canberra replacement as it would cut down costs, since only a single type would need to be developed.

Given that there was no love lost between the two services, the RAF declined to join in the Buccaneer programme, deciding to push onward with the BAC TSR-2, Tactical Strike Reconnaissance Mach 2. The deadline for submissions was January 1958. Official opinions of the English Electric proposal found it decidedly lacking in comparison to the Vickers entry; however, the combination of the two was felt by officialdom to be a good marriage, thus the development contract was awarded to Vickers with English Electric as the primary sub-contractor.

In January 1959 the Minister of Supply announced that the TSR-2 would be built by Vickers, working in conjunction with English Electric. The TSR-2 was to be powered by two Bristol Siddeley Olympus reheated turbojets – advanced versions of those used in the Avro Vulcan. The design featured a small shoulder-mounted delta wing with down-turned outer panels, an all-moving swept tailplane and a large all-moving fin. Blown flaps were fitted across the entire trailing edge of the wing to achieve the short take-off and landing. No ailerons were fitted with control in roll instead being implemented by differential movement of the slab tailplanes. The wing loading was high for its time, enabling the aircraft to fly at very high speed and low level with great stability. The aircraft featured some extremely sophisticated avionics for navigation and weapons delivery; this would also prove to be one of the reasons for the increasing costs. These systems were coupled to an autopilot system that allowed long-distance terrain-following sorties as crew workload and pilot input were greatly reduced.

Unlike most previous projects, there were to be no prototypes. Under the development batch procedure pioneered by the Americans, there would be a development batch of nine airframes built using production standard jigs. The choice of proceeding to production tooling turned out to be another source of delay, with the first aircraft having to adhere to strict production standards or deal with the hassle of attaining concessions to allow them to exhibit differences from later airframes. Despite the increasing costs, the first two of the development batch aircraft were completed. Engine and undercarriage problems led to delays to the first flight, which meant that the TSR-2 missed the opportunity to be displayed at that year's Farnborough Airshow.

Test pilot Roland Beamont finally made the first flight from the A&AEE at Boscombe Down on 27 September 1964. Initial flight tests were all performed with the undercarriage down and engine power limited on this short flight. On the tenth test flight the landing gear successfully retracted, problems having prevented this on previous occasions, but serious vibration problems on landing persisted throughout the flight testing programme. The first supersonic test flight was achieved on the transfer from Boscombe Down to Warton. During the flight, the aircraft achieved Mach 1 on dry power only.

Over a period of six months a total of twenty-four flights were conducted. Most of the complex electronics were not fitted to the first aircraft, so these flights were all concerned with the basic handling, which was deemed outstanding. Speeds of Mach 1.12 and sustained low-level flights down to 200 feet were achieved. The last test flight took place on 31 March 1965.

The BAC TSR-2 was the great white hope for the British aircraft industry. However, unrealistic costs for the project and their over-runs led to the cancellation of the entire programme. (NARA via Dennis R. Jenkins)

TSR2 XR222 was the fourth prototype and was nearly complete when the programme was cancelled. Although incomplete, the aircraft moved first to Cranfield then to Duxford, where it was given a full refurbishment. (AviPix)

Due to rising costs and technical delays it was decided to cancel the TSR-2 and obtain an option agreement instead to acquire up to 110 F-111 aircraft with no commitment to buy. Unfortunately for the RAF, the F-111 was suffering problems with the wing sweep mechanism; this would cause a long-term delay to Australian deliveries, while those already in use with the Americans were grounded after some had crashed during operations over Vietnam.

Eventually the Royal Air Force would receive the Buccaneer S.2 anyway.

Did you know?

After the TSR-2 debacle Britain entered into a series of multinational aircraft that produced the Sepecat Jaguar, Panavia Tornado and to some extent the F-4 Phantom, as used by the RAF and the Royal Navy.

11
What Next?

A great way to get a better idea of what these machines are like is to visit one of the several excellent aviation museums in the UK. The best places to see some of these mighty beasts include:

Bruntingthorpe Aviation Museum, Leicestershire
One of the few places where Cold War-era jets can be heard as well as seen. On open days it is possible to see a fast-taxiing Buccaneer, Hunter, Lightning and Victor, among other types.
www.bruntingthorpeaviation.com/

Fleet Air Arm Museum, Yeovilton, Somerset
This museum houses numerous rare examples of Royal Navy aircraft. It is also home to the British Concorde prototype and the Fairey FD2 that tested the Concorde wing planform.
http://www.fleetairarm.com/

Imperial War Museum, Duxford, Cambridgeshire
This extensive aviation museum includes one of the two TSR-2 prototypes, and numerous other types covered by this book, including the Vulcan, Lightning and Canberra.
http://www.iwm.org.uk/visits/iwm-duxford

National Museum of Flight, East Fortune, East Lothian
The collection here includes the oldest surviving Harrier, a Sea Hawk, Lightning, Buccaneer, Vulcan and Meteor night fighter.
www.nms.ac.uk/national-museum-of-flight

Newark Air Museum, Nottinghamshire
A good proportion of all types covered may be found in this smaller museum that has an emphasis on post-war British military aviation.
www.newarkairmuseum.org

RAF Museum, Cosford, Shropshire
The northern outpost of the RAF Museum, this building complex houses numerous prototypes and a complete example of the BAC TSR-2. It is home of the National Cold War Exhibition.
www.rafmuseum.org.uk/cosford/

RAF Museum, Hendon, London
Home to many rare examples of RAF aircraft restored to a beautiful standard. The Vulcan here required some interesting dismantling and reassembly techniques to get it into the building.
www.rafmuseum.org.uk/london/

Robin Hood Airport, Doncaster
The former RAF Finningley is now home to Vulcan XH558, now unfortunately grounded after several years entertaining the crowds at air shows around the country. Canberra WK163 is now being restored to fly by the Vulcan team.
www.vulcantothesky.org/

Air Shows
It is possible to see a number of the types featured in this book perform at air shows around the country. Sadly, the Vulcan that delighted crowds for several years is now grounded indefinitely, but some of the smaller types – possibly including the Vampire, Venom, Sea Vixen, Meteor, Canberra and Hunter – are represented on the air show circuit. For details go to britishairshows.com.

Further reading
There are countless books available covering the post-war products of the British aircraft industry, and military types are particularly well covered. What follows is a very small selection of books that expand upon the story you have just read.

Bond, Steven J., *Meteor: Gloster's First Jet Fighter* (Midland Publishing, 1985)
Written by my old friend Steve Bond, this slender tome covers the Meteor story in depth, including a history of every aircraft built.

Burke, Damien, *TSR2: Britain's Lost Bomber* (Crowood Press, 2010)
Probably the best book on the doomed TSR2 project.

Darling, Kev, *Avro Vulcan* (Crowood Press, 2005)
Having spent eleven years involved with the Vulcan at many levels of servicing, the author covers in great depth the lives of the aircrew and ground crew and the aircraft they flew.

Darling, Kev, *Blackburn Buccaneer* (Crowood Press, 2006)

Darling, Kev, *Fleet Air Arm Carrier War* (Pen & Sword, 2009)
This mighty tome by yours truly covers the history of the Fleet Air Arm up to 2008, covering the aircraft mentioned within these covers in great depth.

Darling, Kev, *Lightning: The Operational History* (Airlife, 1995)

Hamilton-Paterson, James, *Empire of the Clouds – When Britain's Aircraft Ruled the World* (Faber & Faber, 2010)
The story of the great years, and the decline, of the British aviation industry, with all its successes, and failures.

Mason, Francis K., *Hawker Hunter: Biography of a Thoroughbred* (Patrick Stephens, 1985)
Although quite an old book it is re-issued at regular intervals, as its coverage of the Hunter's development is second to none.

Morgan, Eric B., *Vickers Valiant: The First V-bomber* (Aerofax, 2002)
The late Eric Morgan discovered numerous unknown facts about the Valiant. Containing a history of every airframe built, this is possibly the ultimate Valiant book.

Modelling

Another great way to 'get involved' with the subject is through collecting or building models. Miniature replicas of the aircraft featured in this book have been around since those aircraft were new, and vintage die-casts by Dinky and others, and construction kits by companies including Airfix, Frog and Keil Kraft, are now very collectable.

Modern models in various forms are widely available, in a bewildering range of variants. Pre-assembled collector's models are made by companies including Corgi and Oxford Diecast, but for those who like to get more involved there are hundreds of construction kits in a variety of scales. Clubs up and down the country exist to promote and support aircraft modelling in plastic. There is also a flourishing community of builders constructing flying models of these aircraft from kits or plans. For the very experienced and deep of pocket there are even miniature turbojets available to power these craft!

For plastic modelling a good place to go for support and guidance is the International Plastic Modellers Society (ipmsuk.org), while inspiration regarding larger flying models might be gained from the British Model Flying Association (bmfa.org) or any of its member clubs. As well as a host of web pages and books on the topic, there is also a number of magazines available covering the various sizes and types of model aircraft.